C000231284

Contents

ACKNOWLEDGEMENTS

Photographs are reproduced by kind permission of: Keith Ellis (page 9), the United Reformed Church (pages 12, 34), Radio Times Hulton Picture Library (pages 21, 47) and The Council for World Mission (pages 42 and 44).

COVER PHOTOGRAPH: *The joint meeting of the two assemblies, which brought the United Reformed Church into being by their vote. By courtesy of the United Reformed Church.*

Foreword

The Editors chose wisely in asking Kenneth Slack to describe the United Reformed Church, and to set it in its historical and contemporary context. Apart from his always fluent pen, he was equipped for this task by his intimate knowledge of the steps by which union between Congregationalists and Presbyterians was achieved, by his subsequent service as the Moderator of the first full Assembly of the new Church, and by his present chairmanship of the Church Life Department.

He was himself a foretaste of the union. A Presbyterian up to 1967, he was then called to be minister of the City Temple and moved over on to the roll of the Congregational Church. His earlier service as Secretary of the British Council of Churches gave him a deep and sensitive knowledge of all the Churches as is revealed in his *British Churches Today*.

The subject of this book is a comparatively small Church, but a Church which inherits important Christian traditions, and one which is the representative in England of the world-wide family of Reformed Churches. It is a Church unique in Britain because it was born out of the first act of union across the confessional divides to have happened in these islands since the Reformation. While the issues that had to be resolved, in order to bring about the Union, mainly concerned questions of Church Order, these are vital spiritual questions about how Christ can live in and guide his Church. They touch deep differences in human understanding and arose out of the most creative conflicts in British history.

If the new Church here so well described can resolve the living tensions that it has inherited, it will have profound things to say both about unity and about freedom and order in society. I gladly commend this book as a guide to an important part of the Church life of Britain, written by an expert who is so much part of its present witness that what he writes is alive with interests and issues that will affect the Churches for years to come.

Arthur L. Macarthur
General Secretary, United Reformed Church

1

A
Coming
Together

The autumn of 1972 must have been a busy time for the people who do sign-writing for church notice-boards and make those enamel plaques that are fixed on to lamp-posts to direct you to a particular building. About two thousand churches, mostly in England but with quite a few in Wales (all, however, English-speaking), were getting a new name. That name was 'The United Reformed Church'. It is important to note the 'ed' at the end of 'Reformed'. It is often missed off, and people get confused with a group of Jewish synagogues which use the title without the 'ed'.

When those new titles were put on boards and signs, often there was another title put underneath in brackets. So the full description read 'United Reformed Church (Congregational/Presbyterian)'. Here in fact was the clue: the names in brackets told you who it was that had united to form the new Church. It was the Churches until then known by the names 'Presbyterian' and 'Congregational'. To give them their full names, they were the Congregational Church in England and Wales and the Presbyterian Church of England.

The day of union was 5 October 1972. The great acts of union took place in the morning and the afternoon in the City of Westminster, and in the evening in the City of London. The evening event was more informal and was especially intended as a celebration by young people. It was held in the historic Congregational church, the City Temple. Donald Swann played and sang, there was a pop group and dancing in the aisles to the song 'Day by Day' from *Godspell*. Pictures were flashed on to a large screen, and voices spoke over the loudspeakers.

Why should young people have been excited about the coming together of two Christian denominations? And why did many of the pictures flashed on the screen seem to have little to do with Churches uniting? They were about war, and conflict, and racial strife in many parts of the world. Why was all this human disunity getting mixed up with church unity?

THE IMPORTANCE OF UNITY Perhaps the answer can be seen by looking at the place where the actual act of union happened earlier that day. The official representatives of the two Churches packed the Westminster Central Hall (opposite Westminster Abbey) that morning, to pass the essential formal resolutions that made two Churches one, and set up the basic machinery for the new Church's life. The Central Hall houses a Methodist church, but it is also used for many great gatherings. On the outside wall can be seen a small plaque which tells of a very important meeting there. It says that the first Assembly of the United Nations met there from 10 January to 14 February 1946. Here, in other words, began the tremendous task of trying to bring the whole world into greater unity, straight after the most destructive war ever known. To suggest that there was any connection between that and the union of two quite small Christian denominations in this island may seem at

8

The City Temple.

first far-fetched. The connection might seem only on the surface – that they happened under the same roof. In fact it goes far deeper than that. Despite the terrible wars of the twentieth century, mankind has been seeking unity as never before. This is chiefly because the dangers, if we do not learn to live together, are so terrifying. In the same way the Churches right through this century have been trying to find their lost unity in a movement called 'the ecumenical movement'. The word 'ecumenical' comes from a Greek word meaning 'the whole inhabited earth'. So the search for Christian unity is not just a 'churchy' business. It has to do with all mankind being one.

The British Churches and their leaders have played a great part in this unity movement across the world. A good number of foreign Churches which came into being because of the missionary work of the British Churches have now united – as in South India in 1947, and, more recently, in North India. The startling fact is that until that October morning in 1972 there had never been a single union of two different kinds of Church in the whole of British history!

Churches belonging to the same 'family' of Churches had certainly come together. Those who read the books in this series on the Church of Scotland and the Methodist Church will discover that. In 1929 two great Presbyterian Churches came together to form the Church of Scotland as it is today. Three years later three divided parts of the Methodist family were united to form today's Methodist Church. These were very important unions which created very great Churches. But in another sense they were easy unions, for they only brought together in the first case Presbyterian Churches and in the second Methodist Churches. Could union happen between different kinds of Church? That was the crucial question. The answer that came that October morning in 1972 did not come with a great roar from the throats of many Churches, but it did come as a firm and clear cry from two – and it was 'Yes'.

It was a great moment for British Christianity, and this was shown by the presence of Dr Ramsey, the then Archbishop of Canterbury. It was even a significant moment for world Christianity, for it suggested that the British Churches were no longer just going to watch Churches elsewhere unite – and this was symbolised by the presence of Dr Eugene Carson Blake, who was then the General Secretary of the World Council of Churches. Most important, it was one more bit of concrete evidence that the Church of Jesus Christ has some right to claim that in Jesus there was the power to overcome the deep divisions within mankind that cause so much destruction and misery. After all, as long as people can point to disunited Churches they can fairly easily scoff at this big claim. There is a story that in the Kremlin there was a most impressive doorway bearing an even more impressive title, 'Commissar for Electrification of All the Russias'. It looked far less impressive when a bit of paper was stuck under it, which read 'Bell out of order: please knock'. For far too long the Churches have been like that: they make very big claims but do not demonstrate how they work.

Every act of Christian unity is therefore some demonstration that it is possible for very different people to come together to help and enrich each other. This is a message our world needs desperately, and the young people who danced in the aisles of the City Temple were celebrating something that mattered for human unity.

But it was only a very small step. The two Churches that made the United Reformed Church that day, declared at the moment of union that the new Church wanted to enter into wider unions:

> The United Reformed Church declares its intention, in fellowship with all the Churches, to pray and work for such visible unity of the whole Church as Christ wills and in the way he wills, in order that men and nations may be led more and more to glorify the Father in heaven.

The service of thanksgiving in Westminster Abbey. Dr Huxtable receives the promise of the Archbishop of Canterbury to share in the search for wider unity. Cardinal Heenan watches before making the promise himself.

In the afternoon of the great day the assembly of the new Church made its way across the road to Westminster Abbey to thank God for his gift of unity. In that service the most memorable moments were when the Archbishop of Canterbury, the Cardinal Archbishop of Westminster and the Moderator of the Free Church Federal Council, on behalf of all the Churches, solemnly welcomed what had been done and promised to share in the exploring of the unity that Christ wills.

The coming into being of the United Reformed Church was only one step in the search among the British Churches for the kind of unity that people can see; but it *was* a step, and a firm and definite one.

Think about . . .

Try to find out about the various ways in which the Churches in your area have been coming together in the movement towards unity. Find out if there is a Council of Churches and what it does.

Keep your eyes open in May each year to see Christian Aid Week in operation. You will see posters on the hoardings. There may be a door-to-door collection. Perhaps there will be sponsored walks or swims and other events. Christian Aid demonstrates the way the Churches work together for needy people right across the world – refugees, victims of disaster and most of all the poor and hungry. This is part of the great unity movement. Do you think that it is important for Churches to work together in various relief organisations? Does this sort of co-operation improve people's opinion of the Churches?

Look around your town to see if there is a United Reformed Church, and find out what kind of Church it was before 1972.

The Two Different Churches

Unlike the other books in this series this one is about a united Church, and it must therefore tell something of the story of the two Churches that make it up. What, in fact, is the meaning of the phrase in brackets on those church notice-boards 'Congregational/Presbyterian'? The fact that we have to study two stories, and have no more space than the other books, means that we can only sketch the history and character of the two Churches very much in outline.

THE REFORMATION   Both Churches arose from the Reformation. That is recorded in the new name 'The United *Reformed* Church' in England and Wales. Both, too, arose from the same side of the Reformation, that linked with the name of John Calvin, the Frenchman who did his great work in the Swiss city of Geneva.

There were two main sides of the Reformation. One came from the work of Martin Luther. This had its biggest influence on the continent of Europe, as you can see in the great Lutheran

Churches of Luther's native country, Germany, and of the Scandinavian lands. Lutheranism also (less directly) affected the Church of England. Much later, Lutheranism flowed into English Christianity in a different way, through John and Charles Wesley with their great love of Lutheran hymns which they put into English.

Luther put great stress on what Christ did for the human heart, bringing a man into peace and harmony with God. He was not much concerned to alter the shape of the Church itself, as long as that shape did not get in the way of the man whose spirit yearned to come to God through Christ. He was, for example, content to leave ritual unchanged unless it involved something that the Bible actually forbade.

Calvin was a very different man. He believed that the Church as it then was needed most drastic re-forming ('reformation') after the pattern of the New Testament Church. Nothing should enter the worship which did not find actual authority in scripture. That meant that worship must be plain and simple. The minister was not to be seen as a priest saying mass, but first and foremost as a teacher of the Word of God. That meant that he must be properly trained. Then he must train his people. The ordinary people, the laity, were to be able to understand Scripture and to base their lives upon it. There was to be no distinction between the 'religious life' – meaning monks, nuns and friars – and people working in the world. Everybody had a 'calling'; that meant a calling from God to serve him in daily life. The clerk in the counting-house, the merchant in his shop, the maid in the scullery – all in any honourable work were fulfilling their calling. They were offering God their best service. You can see straight away what a new dignity and worth this gave to ordinary Christians.

But if they gained that dignity and worth, much was also expected of them. The church was no longer somewhere you went to hear the mass murmured in the distance by the priest. It was to be a fellowship of right-living people, and arrangements had to be made to ensure that it became such and remained such. Elders were to be chosen. These were men still employed in their ordinary work but set apart for spiritual duties in the government of the church. That government included discipline for the sinner, not just seeing that the church machinery ran smoothly. The church, in fact, was to be a place where men were made Christian and kept Christian.

People usually associate the name of John Calvin with predestination. Certainly that doctrine loomed large in the story of the churches he founded. It was that God had pre-destined (intended) some people to be saved and some to be damned. At its worst it was an appalling doctrine, and taken literally would have stopped anyone trying to evangelise, that is, make other people Christian. What would be the point, if God had already decided things beforehand?

But in fact predestination was only really the too logical working out of the teaching that was the very heart of Calvin's message. That teaching was that God was sovereign: he must be sovereign in the lives of the men and women that made up his Church. It was often rather harshly expressed, but it was a bracing teaching that made for strong churches and strong Christians. It is not just coincidence that Calvinist Christianity has supplied some of the toughest and most courageous missionaries and other heroes of the Christian story. If a man believes that God is sovereign over all things, and over his own life, he is able to face great difficulties and sufferings with a brave heart. The modern Congregational and Presbyterian Churches were not, and the United Reformed Church is not, strong on predestination. It finds no place in the basis of the United Reformed Church. But it would be a pity if the new Church did not strongly hold the doctrine that God – the God and Father of Jesus Christ – is sovereign over his Church and world.

Although both our two Churches – Congregational and Presbyterian – come from the Calvinist side of the Reformation, they parted company quite early in the story. In the British Isles the most influential figure in the development of Presbyterian churchmanship was John Knox. Not all his work, by any means, was done in Scotland. But it is right that we should chiefly link his name with that country. He and his successors there did so strong a work that the national Church north of the Border became Presbyterian, as it remains to this day (see the book in the present series on the Church of Scotland). More than this, all English-speaking Presbyterianism throughout the world – in the U.S.A., the British dominions and elsewhere – comes from that work of Knox and his successors.

PRESBYTERIAN ORGANISATION In that kind of Presbyterianism, to which the Presbyterian Church of England belonged, the re-formed Church was centralised. (We shall see more clearly what that means when we come to Congregationalism, which was decentralised). In this form of Church, the local congregation is seen as the expression, in a particular place, of a whole Church throughout the nation. This whole Church, by its structure and machinery, holds everything together and exercises some real measure of control or government over all the local congregations.

You may wonder how in fact this differed from what had been there before Calvin did his work. The local parish was part of a diocese with its bishop, and the diocese was part of a province, or national Church, with its archbishop, and those Churches were part of a whole Church which looked to the Pope of Rome as its head. The answer is that while in one sense it did not differ, in another sense it differed very profoundly indeed.

It did not differ in the sense that the Church must be seen clearly as one, with an authority that held it together. Where it differed profoundly was in the way in which that authority was exercised, and, even more, who exercised it.

In a Presbyterian Church there are no bishops, and (of course) no Pope. All authority is exercised by courts or councils of the Church. The local congregation is governed by a session, which is composed of the minister and the elders. Then the churches in a region are governed by a presbytery. But this presbytery consists of representatives, ministers and elders, from all the local congregations in the area. Then nationally the Church is governed by a general assembly. This in turn is made up of ministers and elders from local congregations.

So the picture of the Church as one, but spread through many local places, is the same whether you are talking of the kind of Church that has bishops (like the Church of England) or a Presbyterian Church. One has a hierarchy of individuals, the other of Church councils or courts. There is one big difference; in the Presbyterian system the voice of the local congregation at the decision-making points is a very real one. (But it is a measure of how we are all growing together that the government of the Church of England, through its General Synod, now has a strongly Presbyterian element in it).

CONGREGATIONAL ORGANISATION   The Congregational system was wholly different. Unless you appreciate this it is not easy to see what a big step the formation of the United Reformed Church was. Put simply, although Congregationalists, or – to give them their old name – Independents, believed quite as strongly that the Church should be reformed, they also believed that the pattern should be very different indeed. They believed that Christ must reign in his Church: they were certainly heirs to John Calvin in that. But they thought that this should not be expressed in Presbyterianism's series of Church courts, but by Christ's reign in every fellowship of believers who gathered together in his name. Far from the final authority being in a general assembly of the Churches of the nation, it was to be found in any simple local fellowship which sought to know the mind of Christ. There could be no authority beyond that.

This kind of Independency or Congregationalism was a particularly English kind of churchmanship, though it has spread to many parts of the world, both by missionary work and by the emigration of people who held the faith in that way. Probably the most famous of those emigrations is that of the Pilgrim Fathers in their little ship the *Mayflower*. They were Congregationalists, and they greatly influenced the early days of the American colonies that became the United States of America.

NONCONFORMISTS IN ENGLAND   In the reigns of Elizabeth I, James I and Charles I there was a Presbyterian party at work within the Church of England, trying to change the national Church from within, from its Anglican form, with bishops, to the model set up by John Calvin in Geneva and by John Knox in Scotland. The Episcopalians and the Presbyterians for all their bitter differences were agreed on one thing – that the Christian Church, and the Christian nation in which it was set, were really one and the same thing. The church was the nation, as it were, on its religious side.

The Independents, or Congregationalists (to give them their more modern name), disagreed. Like the Baptists (see the book on them in this series) they believed that Christians were not just all the people of a so-called Christian country who happened to have been baptized as babies, but only those who had fully and responsibly offered themselves to God. People like that were seen as having made a 'covenant' to form a church in a particular place. 'Covenanting' meant making not only a promise to each other but also a promise to Christ. They promised to be his church in that town or village. That kind of church was often called a 'gathered' church. That meant that it was not just all the people living in the parish, but only those whom God had gathered together specially to be his people.

The first man really to work out these ideas was an Englishman, Robert Browne. He lived from around 1550 until 1633. He taught that every Christian in that kind of gathered church had his place and responsibility within it. That sounds like a very democratic recipe, and it is certainly true that Congregationalism made a special contribution to democracy in our national politics. But that was not what Browne was really after. He was concerned not that everybody should have a voice but that everybody should listen to what Christ wanted his church to be and do. Browne was not himself a very important man, like, say, John Knox or John Wesley. What he chiefly did was to set down in writing the thoughts and ideas that were already at work in that exciting time we call the Reformation.

But it was the pastor of the congregation in Leyden, in Holland, where early Independents had gone to be free to worship God in the kind of church in which they had come to believe, who put into some famous words the real heart of this kind of churchmanship. His name was John Robinson, and the occasion when he spoke the words was a historic one. It was when the tiny *Mayflower* set sail on its dangerous journey across the Atlantic:

> I charge you, before God and his blessed angels, that you follow me no further than you have seen me follow the Lord Jesus Christ. If God reveal anything to you by any other instrument of his, be as ready to receive it as you were to receive any truth by my ministry, for I am verily persuaded the Lord hath more truth yet to break forth out of his holy word.... The Calvinists, you see, stick fast where they were left by the great man of God, who yet saw not all things.

John Robinson's words were wonderfully tolerant for those days, when people were apt to persecute those who were not of their own religious opinions. Note, too, how progressive they are. The 'Calvinists' he is speaking of are

Oliver Cromwell.

the Presbyterians. He sees them as having got stuck with their founder, and not ready to see that God was always causing *new* light to break out of his word.

In the terrible struggle which was to come in the English Civil War, and in the Commonwealth that followed, the Congregationalists were generally on the side of tolerance. For all that, they produced from their own company the Lord Protector himself, Oliver Cromwell, who perhaps was not intolerant, but who cannot be thought very democratic. They also produced one of the greatest of English poets, John Milton.

When the Commonwealth came to an end and Charles II came to his throne an Act of Uniformity was passed, and all who could not accept the restoring of the old kind of Church, the Church of England with its bishops, had to leave. Presbyterians, Baptists and Congregationalists were forced out, and it is from 1662 when that Act of Parliament was passed that the Free Churches, or the 'nonconformists' (to give them their old title) can be dated. Over 1600 ministers were ejected from their churches because they would not 'conform'. Very harsh restrictions followed upon these ministers and those of their flocks who followed them. They were not allowed to meet within five miles of any town having a corporation, and were driven to all kinds of heroic tricks to get warning of the approach of the constables to break up the meetings for worship.

It is sad to record that Presbyterianism very largely disappeared under these conditions which went on for a long time. Many Presbyterians lost their orthodox faith and became Unitarians, that is, they no longer believed that Jesus Christ was the unique Son of God. Of course, there were very real difficulties in keeping a Presbyterian system going, with the necessary meetings of the courts of the Church, when every gathering was spied on and virtually prohibited. But the same circumstances fitted the Congregationalists quite well. The very fact that their system put all the responsibility for church government finally on the local church meant that you could keep going so long as you could meet in some way for worship and fellowship. As time went on it became possible to get a licence for a meeting-house for nonconformist worship. A 'gathered' church with such a licence could be everything which a church ought to be according to Congregational principles. It was an excellent system for times of persecution and restriction.

GROWING TOGETHER   By the time the nineteenth century came the situation was becoming far happier. To start with, there were many more people who did not conform to the Church of England – all the people called Methodists. A new spirit of toleration was beginning. Many people in Congregational churches were becoming wealthy and having more importance and influence. They were traders and merchants, and manufacturers in wool and cotton and other goods. Presbyterianism began to appear again on the English scene, partly because the industrial revolution caused people to move about far more: Scots and people from Ulster came to parts of England, and most of them were Presbyterians. Half way through the previous century presbyteries had been formed again in Newcastle upon Tyne and in Northumberland, for that form of churchmanship had never really died out in the north-east of England. Presbyteries gradually grew up elsewhere, such as in Lancashire and London. In 1844 the decision was made to form a Presbyterian Church in England. It had only seventy congregations. A good number of congregations that were in England, but were made up of Scots, kept their connection with Scotland. Then in 1876 they all came together. Now there were over 250 congregations and the name 'The Presbyterian Church *of* England' was taken, to declare that it meant to be not a Church chiefly for Scottish exiles, but a Church with a place in English life.

It was this Presbyterian Church of England – still not large, with only some 70 000 members and 330 churches – which was to lose its life almost a hundred years later in the United Reformed Church.

In the nineteenth century the Congregational churches had known considerable change, too. This was notably in a closer drawing together of the independent churches. In any case it would be wrong to caricature the degree to which these churches were 'independent' of one another. 'County Unions' began to be formed in the eighteenth century and became far stronger in the nineteenth. These consisted of the churches within a particular county, such as Lancashire and Somerset. Members, both ministers and lay people, came to meetings representing all the churches of the county. Those meetings, or assemblies, did not have any power or control over the local churches. What they could do was to inspire them, to help them and to give them a sense of belonging to something far bigger than the local church.

In 1832 a national union was formed, the Congregational Union of England and Wales. (The churches in Wales that belonged to it were the English-speaking churches: the Welsh-speaking churches belonged – as they still do – to the Union of Welsh Independents.) The Congregational Union in England and Wales became increasingly important as the years went by. Its annual assembly to which representatives, again both ministers and lay people, could come from every church, became very influential and gave to the Congregational churches a truly national voice. The headquarters of the union stood on the site of a prison in the old City of London where many members of the Congregational churches had suffered imprisonment for their faith in earlier intolerant days. It was called Memorial Hall to commemorate this fact. Sadly it is no longer there; not many years ago it was knocked down and replaced by a modern block of offices. Nevertheless, it had its place in our country's history, for it was at a meeting held there that the decision was first made to form the Labour Party.

The possession of a central office and a succession of very able leaders working in it did much to draw together the churches throughout the country for all kinds of purposes. Not many years before the formation of the United Reformed Church the Congregational Union underwent a big change. In 1966 it became the Congregational Church in England and Wales. Earlier Congregationalists would not have liked this. They stressed that the power of the church was finally in the local congregation, and no wider grouping should call itself a 'Church'. But, more reasonably as many

24

of us would think, in recent years the question began to be asked – if Christians can 'covenant' together to form a local church why cannot local churches in various places covenant together to be the Church of a nation?

You can see that all these moves gradually made it possible for union with the Presbyterian Church of England to be achieved more easily. In that Church, too, there had been changes. Just because Presbyterians believe in the way of Church government which binds all churches closely together, they have a real temptation to be rather rigid and attach too much importance to law and authority. Again, in English Presbyterianism there has been a temptation to look towards Scotland where the national Church is Presbyterian, and not bother enough about really belonging to *English* life.

Both these tendencies lessened as this century went by. 'Bossiness' in Presbyterianism was reduced. And the role that the Presbyterian Church played in many new areas which were built up between the two world wars, often becoming the local Free Church for everybody, made the Church more English than perhaps it had been.

UNION Even then the union of the two Churches did not prove easy. A vigorous attempt was made to achieve it straight after the Second World War. A lot of work was put into the attempt for years. It failed. But slowly the two Churches grew together, and early in the 1960s it was resolved to try again.

In fact it took nine years to bring the union about. This sounds a long time. It was necessary for two reasons. When two bodies with a long history are going to cease to exist, and a new body comes into being in their place, there is a lot to be done. You have to work out how to unite at very many levels. How is the the new Church, for example, to do its missionary work overseas? Is the Congregational way or the Presbyterian way to be followed in this or that

25

matter where the two happen to differ? The sheer weight of work to be done accounts partly for the time taken. But the second reason is that every stage of the plan for union had to be submitted to the people of the two Churches. This was so that it could be discussed not only at the national assemblies (which only meet once a year) but right throughout the country wherever churches and congregations were to be found. As great a decision as that demanded such wide discussion. More that that, you will have seen that only if that discussion took place locally was it possible for the Congregationalists especially to unite. That was where the power of decision finally lay.

There was one last complication that took up some time. It may seem an odd happening. There had to be an Act of Parliament to enable the union to take place! But, you may say, surely these were two *Free* Churches; they weren't connected with the State in the way the Church of England is. That is true, but any Church, or any charitable body, which holds any property or money has one big difficulty to face when they want to make a great change. It is that the property and funds are held 'on trust' for particular stated purposes – in this case, for Congregational or Presbyterian purposes. Supposing when the union happened a small group of people who did not agree with it said, 'We claim the whole of the church buildings and funds, because we are still Congregationalists'. Without the Act of Parliament that authorised the change they might have won their case. (Something like this actually happened in Scotland in 1900.)

The Act of Parliament only said that *if* the two Churches united then the trusts could be changed. The decision was a free one for the Churches to make. They made it, and by large majorities decided to come together – although some Congregational churches chose to do otherwise. Needless to say, those churches have been treated very generously with regard to property and funds.

But, as we have already seen, by October 1972 the Act

was passed and the resolutions to unite were agreed. Two Churches died and a new one lived.

Is there a church in your area which was Congregational or Presbyterian? If there is a Congregational church and it has been there for a long time it may have the old name somewhere about it, 'Independent Chapel'. Find out what county union it belonged to, or, in the case of a Presbyterian church, what presbytery.

If your parish church is old and has a board in it with the names of all the rectors or vicars, look round about 1662 and see if the clergyman then is described as 'ejected', i.e. put out. That would mean that he may have been a Congregationalist or a Presbyterian. The local library may be able to help you find out if afterwards he met with worshippers of his kind elsewhere. In fact the local history part of the library would help you to trace, in your own locality, the kind of church history that this short book is about.

Think about the effect that the kind of churchmanship described in this chapter will have had on the people who took part in it. What effect do you think these sort of religious movements had on the development of modern democratic Britain?

3

The Shape
of the
New Church

What was the new Church like, that came into being on that October day in 1972? Did belonging to it make any very big changes for the people who just belonged to their local church, joined in its worship and took some part in its life?

The first impression might have been that it did not. For one thing, the two Churches were very like one another in their ways of worship. Neither, for example, used a fixed form of service, like the Roman Catholic Church or the Church of England. The minister might draw his prayers from many sources, but no service book was put into the hands of the ordinary worshipper. Perhaps, if anything, Presbyterian churches were rather more formal. You could be certain that the minister, for example, would be robed in black cassock and black gown with white bands or tabs beneath his clerical collar. His rather sombre appearance might be relieved by the colour of the hood of his university degree. Congregational ministers often wore just the same clothes, but some would just wear a gown, and some only their ordinary clothes, without even a clerical collar.

This last-named custom arose during the nineteenth century and early in the present one. It was to stress that the minister is not a priest, and therefore ought not to look as though he is cut off from his fellow Christians. There was a famous *Punch* cartoon of a very well-known Congregational minister who had said in an unwise moment, 'I shall wear no clothes to separate me from my lay brethren'. You can guess how the cartoonist showed him!

But, these outward differences apart, there was little difference in the ways of worship of the two churches. Both treasured the sermon in worship, seeing it as an essential way of producing a properly taught church. (See what is written about Calvin in the last chapter.) Both treasured the right of the minister to offer prayers which lifted the events and needs of the world to God in words which were related to people's ordinary lives. It did not matter whether the minister (as most often in the past) just used the words given to him at the moment, or prepared his prayers beforehand for that purpose, using his own words or the words of others that were found suitable.

One pattern of worship would be followed in both Churches. Prayers adoring God, asking for his pardon for wrongdoing, giving him thanks and asking for his help for ourselves and for the world would be there Sunday by Sunday, but they would not be the same prayers. Readings of scripture, and the explanation of the meaning of parts of the Bible in the sermon, would also be important. Both Churches were alike in this, and this kind of worship continues in the new Church.

BAPTISM They were generally alike, too, in their ways of observing or celebrating the two sacraments of baptism and communion. Baptism, which marks being received into the whole Church, was given to the children of parents who

29

believed in Jesus Christ and belonged to his Church. It showed that such a child, being born into a home that was part of the Church, was in a real sense born into the Church. This sacrament was normally observed (in both Churches) when the whole congregation was present at morning service. The Church is people, not a building: so the Church must be there when a new member is admitted.

The new Church follows just the same practice, but there is a rather exciting change in prospect. Earlier we saw that when the new Church came into being it was firmly stated that it was only seen as one stage towards a wider union. On the very day of union one very small but fine denomination in effect asked us if we meant it! They were 'The Churches of Christ', often known in other parts of the world (where they are far stronger) as 'The Disciples'. Two or three of their leaders had sat as observers in the closing stages of our union committee. Now they asked if we were ready to talk about uniting.

As I write, full and detailed plans for that union are before the two churches. We do not yet know what the decision will be. I mention it here for an important reason. The Churches of Christ, like the far larger Baptists (see the book about them in this series), believe that baptism should only be given to people old enough to say for themselves that they commit themselves to following Jesus and accept him as their Saviour. Then such believers are baptised not by sprinkling of water but by going right down into it – 'immersion' as it is called. It is a wonderful symbol of what the New Testament says about becoming a Christian by dying to the old life and rising to a new life with Christ.

If the proposed new union goes forward the Church will still be called the United Reformed Church, but it will be a richer union. It will contain Christians who believe in the baptism of infants and people who believe only in the baptism of believers, but who are both ready to honour each other's convictions.

THE LORD'S SUPPER   In regard to the communion, or Lord's Supper as it was often called in the two Churches which united, there were great similarities, but some differences – one of which has caused some difficulties. In both Churches this sacrament was observed more rarely than in the Roman Catholic Church or Church of England. In Presbyterian Churches it might be only four times a year, and would rarely be more than eight times. The four great 'quarterly' communions would be attended by specially large congregations, and were seen as times of new Christian commitment. The Congregational churches rarely had less than a monthly communion service, and often would have two each month, one in the morning and one in the evening.

The picture of such a service was really that of everyone being around the Lord's Table. That wasn't physically possible, but a few Presbyterian churches symbolised it by long white linen runners going down the hymn-book boards in the pews – a kind of extension of the table-cloth. Minister, elders and church members were like the Lord and his disciples gathered at his Supper, hearing his words and asking that Jesus would be present within the service, and taking the bread and wine to be signs of Jesus feeding his people with his spiritual gifts. The bread and wine would be taken out by deacons or elders to the members as they sat in their seats, and in many churches they would minister to one another by passing it from hand to hand.

One of the differences was that in most Presbyterian churches only those who were actual Church members – members, that is, of *any* Christian Church – would be invited to receive communion, but in most Congregational churches a more general invitation was given to all who love the Lord Jesus Christ. In Presbyterian churches young people were expected to attend classes of preparation and become members by declaring their Christian faith before they came to communion. Becoming a church member and taking your first communion happened at the same time. In many Congregational churches older children would receive communion for a while before being prepared for church membership, which, of course, in that kind of church gave the privilege of full sharing in the government of the local church.

These differences did not present any great problem. Probably there will be some kind of gradual growing together in the new Church, but possibly many local differences may remain.

MINISTERS   A sharper difference had to be faced before the new Church could come into being. It had to do with who should preside at the Lord's Table. Should it be only an ordained minister – as Presbyterian tradition said – or could it be, when necessary, any member of the congregation appointed to do so, as many Congregational churches believed? Of course, there were far more small Congregational churches in country areas than there were Presbyterian ones. There had never been enough ministers for all these churches. They were also used to having the communion more regularly. If a lay-preacher ministered to such a church with the preaching of the word of God, why should he not preside at the communion? It must be admitted also that there was something of a tradition among some Congregational churches not just that in necessity a layman could preside, but that it was good that he should do so from time to time just to show that the church and not the minister really celebrated the communion.

The new Church made a compromise on this delicate point. Most positively it said that every church, no matter how small, should have some share in the services of a minister. But then it said that there would be need for some others to be authorized to preside to meet the needs of the churches, but that they should be chosen and appointed by the wider Church and not too casually locally.

So when we come back to the opening question of this chapter, concerning the difference that an ordinary worshipper might find, we can still say 'Not a great deal'. But it would certainly be true that if he belonged to a small church which did not too often see a minister, he should see one more often, and might find that it was when that minister came that communion was observed, rather than as in the past when a lay-preacher would be called upon to do so. Or if the worshipper had been a Presbyterian and had never seen a communion service without a minister, he might be faced with an authorised layman, most probably a senior elder, taking that place. So our answer would have to be, 'Not a great number of changes, but some about which there could be strong feelings'. It is not easy to change long-established customs when two Churches become one.

CHURCH MEMBERSHIP That ordinary worshipper if he had been a Presbyterian would face one new demand. He would be expected to come to 'church meeting'. This would be virtually a new experience for him. All the members in his old form of church would be asked to meet just once a year for a kind of business meeting, and if a new minister was being chosen they would be asked to confer about that. But month by month the government of the church would have been wholly carried out by the elders. These were men and women chosen, it is true, by the whole church, and ordained to hold office for life (so long as they stayed in that church), but once chosen they acted and made the decisions.

It was not like that in a Congregational church. As we have seen, Congregationalists believed that every member had a calling to take his part in the government of the church. They had their lay officers, like the Presbyterian elders. These were usually called deacons, and were usually elected for limited terms of service. They might do a lot of work in running the church, but they were accountable to all the members meeting, normally every month, in 'church meeting'.

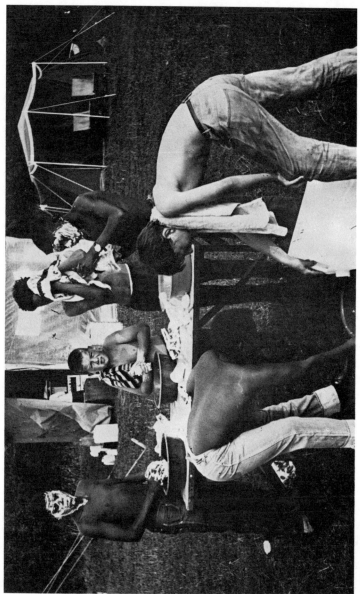

A Boys' Brigade camp.

Nor was the church meeting only concerned with the internal affairs of the church. The church meeting was intended to be a forum where Christians could think about the world and the Christian's duty in it.

We have got to admit that the ideal of the church meeting as the place and time when all members took their common responsibility seriously has never been fully realised. A lot of members failed to take part. It is true today in the new Church, too, but now many people who had belonged to the Presbyterian Church, which did not have it, are finding that it does mean a great deal. It means that the Church of Christ calls for every member to take his responsible part. We hear a lot today, and especially from younger people, about participation in all kinds of government, about not being bossed about by a small number of people, but letting everyone share in the making of decisions. The United Reformed Church is that kind of Church. But it is not just saying that everyone has a say and a vote. It is saying that everyone can discover something of the mind of Christ and share it with his fellow Christians.

CHURCH GOVERNMENT   Locally therefore the new Church has learned much from Congregationalism. In the organisation of the wider Church perhaps the marks of Presbyterianism are seen more. The new district council is more like a presbytery than a county union (see Chapter 2) because it has a real measure of authority. The General Assembly, too, is more like the Presbyterian one than the Congregational. It can make decisions, not just give advice. But at another level the Congregationalists brought a special gift from their experience. Between the district councils and the (national) General Assembly there are synods, which are Church councils that cover a very big area. There are only eleven of them for the whole of England, such as one for all East Anglia, and one for the West Country. Many decisions today call for a look across a wide territory. An example of this is the establishing of New Towns, which will mean new churches and call for a response from the churches across a big area. Each of these twelve synods (there is one for all Wales, too) has a permanent, full-time leader. He is called 'The Moderator of the Province'. The province is the name given to the area a synod cares for.

The Congregational Church had long had provincial moderators. They were ministers with a special job, not a special kind of minister like a bishop. But like a bishop, the moderator's particular task is to care for all the ministers and churches in his area, and to take counsel with his fellow-moderators, especially over such questions as the movement of a minister from one church to another. He cannot decide that. Each local church chooses its own minister, and when a man becomes the minister of that church, his stay there is not limited in years (as it is normally with a Methodist minister). He can decide whether he feels God has called him to the church which invites him. However, in the United Reformed Church there is the precaution that the district council where the inviting church is can decide whether that church is wise to issue the invitation. Again, the district council where the minister's present church is must decide whether he can be spared. So you will see again that in the new Church there is a balance between the responsibility of the local church and the need to look at the needs of the wider Church. The two kinds of church are each bringing their gifts. Congregationalism knew nothing of the say of the wider Church regarding where a minister should serve, but Presbyterianism knew nothing of the help that provincial moderators can give with their personal, caring ministry and ever-growing experience of helping ministers and churches.

These, then, are some of the differences which the ordinary member might find if he were asked to serve in the wider councils of the new Church. This would be more likely to happen if he were chosen to be an elder. (I use 'he' for convenience: all offices in the new Church, as in the two Churches that united, are open without any distinction to men and women. This includes the ordained ministry.) Service as an elder will come to more people in the new Church: a minister is ordained for life, but an elder will only serve for a limited number of years. He may be re-elected, but it is possible that he may not be. This was a deliberate decision, to make sure that 'elder' did not come to mean 'increasingly old'! Some elders are young: I know a girl of twenty-three who is an active elder in a large church.

Some readers may well be thinking that the way Churches are governed is not a very thrilling subject. We can readily agree with them, but still go on to say two things. One is that the biggest way in which the two uniting Churches differed was in Church government, as we have seen in Chapter 2. It may not be thrilling, but people can feel passionately about such things. They prize the freedom they have had, or the system that they think has preserved order. The other thing to be said is that Churches need to be governed in a way that is sensitive to people's need to share in the making of decisions. They must also be governed in a way that is sensitive to the changes in the world that need a swift response. The United Reformed Church is really a rather exciting experiment in balancing the need for shared decision-making with the need for ways of responding to the big changes going on today.

As I write, the new Church has not been in existence for five years. Probably we have not got everything right, for all the nine years of work and discussion before we came together. But this can be said—it is hard to meet anyone who would go back to the old days of separation. Many of the churches which held aloof at the beginning have entered the union now.

Think about . . .

If there is a United Reformed church in your area try to arrange to be shown round it. Note the arrangements of the furniture. Probably the pulpit is prominent: this shows how central the preaching is to worship. The communion table will probably have seats for the minister and elders behind it, showing how the service is conducted. The font for baptisms will be near the pulpit, showing that baptisms are conducted in front of the whole congregation. Note how the church will almost certainly have a number of halls and rooms attached to it. Try to find out about the Christian education work that goes on in them.

Do you think it would be a good thing if all the Christian Churches were able to unite? From what you know of other denominations, do you think it would be possible for them to overcome their differences, such as those concerning communion and baptism? (Consult the other books in this series.)

4

A
Great
Inheritance

At the end of Chapter 2 I wrote of two Churches dying and a new one coming to life. But if we think of it that way, we have to rejoice that the new Church was left everything in the wills of the two that died! Members of the United Reformed Church have entered into a wonderful inheritance.

We have just seen something of this, in the way in which different emphases in Church government have been brought together in a new whole. But the ordinary church member is aware of the inheritance in rather different ways.

I was a Presbyterian, so perhaps I can best write of it by thinking of the things in which I now share. One is the sense of belonging to a Church which is spread virtually throughout the country. English Presbyterianism was only strong is some areas, notably in the northeast, and also in London and on Merseyside. It was only represented by a tiny number of churches in East Anglia and the West Country. Now almost wherever I go I find my own

Church – the United Reformed Church. It is good to belong to a Church which has that stake in the nation's life.

By contrast, I have discovered that former Congregational friends are rather thrilled to belong to a much bigger Church family in the rest of the British Isles. Very emphatically in Scotland, but also in Wales and in Northern Ireland, Presbyterianism is strong. The new Church relates now to a wide family in these islands.

MISSIONARY WORK   But I also feel that now I belong to a bigger family far beyond these islands. This is because of the great spread of the missionary work in which the Congregational churches shared, and some of the great missionary heroes that they produced. This does not mean that the Presbyterian Church of England did not have a fine missionary work, to which it was fully committed as a Church. As well as in a small area in what is now Bangladesh, the English Presbyterians carried out their missionary work among the Chinese, first in southern China and then in the island of Formosa (now called Taiwan) and Malaya.

When the Presbyterian Church *in* England was formed in 1844 one of its very first acts – small though it was – was to establish its own foreign mission. The first missionary, William Chalmers Burns (1815–68), was possibly also the greatest who ever served the mission. He was arrested, set upon by robbers and beaten, and endured many sufferings, very much like St Paul. Like the great apostle, too, nothing was important to him except his call to preach the gospel of Christ. He was a great missionary pioneer, constantly on the move amid many hardships.

Another later missionary of great fame was Thomas Barclay (1849–1935) who served the Church in the lovely island of Formosa for sixty years. If Burns was a pioneering evangelist, Barclay was a great builder of the Church. The Formosan Church became larger than the Presbyterian Church of England which had sent its missionaries to it. Barclay built up great schools and training institutions. He also translated the whole of the Bible into the Amoy dialect, beginning his work on the Old Testament at the ripe age of seventy-eight. He was a true missionary of a Reformed Church with his belief in an educated Church, a well-trained ministry and the Bible open to everybody.

While the Presbyterian Church of England had a fine mission (later much cut down in size when Communist China closed southern China to missionary work), the story of the Congregational share in world mission was even more exciting. If you say the word 'missionary' to most people, probably even today the name of David Livingstone (1813–73) would swiftly leap to their minds. He is perhaps the most famous missionary ever to leave these shores. He left under the auspices of the London Missionary Society, which has been the main instrument for Congregationalism's missionary outreach.

The London Missionary Society was formed in 1795, very early in the modern missionary movement. It was formed by Congregationalists, Anglicans, Presbyterians and Methodists, so it was never just a Congregational society. One way in which its united character was shown was in its declaration that its commitment to the conversion of 'the heathen' did not involve imposing on the churches that came into being overseas any particular form of Church government. But though members of other denominations have served the London Missionary Society both at home and abroad, and Congregationalists in other lands, like Australia, have shared in its work, it has been supremely the missionary organisation of the Congregational churches in England and Wales. (In 1966 its name was changed to the Congregational Council for World Mission; more recently still the word 'congregational' has been dropped.)

The spread of its work has been enormous – China, India, S.E. Asia, southern and East Africa and (rather romantically) the South Sea Islands have all been areas of London Missionary Society activity. Livingstone was the greatest of the exploring, pioneering missionaries, living on a

David Livingstone.

grander scale the kind of life that William Chalmers Burns had lived in China. Both men were men of the Bible, and men of intrepid courage, not concerned chiefly to build up the Church but to break new ground and enter new territories for the gospel. However, Livingstone did build up some institutions, both in medical work and schools. This should not be forgotten in the often-told tale of the explorer being greeted in Victorian style by H. M. Stanley, who had been sent in search of him: 'Dr Livingstone, I presume'. When we entered Westminster Abbey to give God thanks for the formation of the United Reformed Church we crossed Livingstone's tomb. There his body lies, but even more fittingly his heart was buried in Africa.

The most famous pioneer of missionary work in the islands of the South Seas was John Williams (1796–1839). He arrived there in 1817. His great policy was to place native teachers throughout the scattered islands, where it was rarely possible for him to visit. This was a brave policy, for the teachers were new to their Christian faith, but it led to a great growth of the Church throughout the islands, even though some of the teachers became martyrs, dying for their faith. The same fate awaited John Williams. He and a young companion were clubbed and speared to death, and then eaten in a cannibal feast. They were the victims of people who confused these white men with the slave-traders who had recently landed on the island and done their terrible work.

The name of John Williams has stayed alive not only because of his heroic life and martyr's death, but because children of Congregational churches, generation by generation, subscribed and raised money to provide a succession of ships to bear his name and to go on missionary journeys between the islands he served so wonderfully. In the headquarters of the Council for World Mission in Westminster, understandably called Livingstone House, you can see lovely pictures of the John Williams ships, sailing ships, steamers and motor vessels, that have carried on this work.

John Williams VII, *owned by the London Missionary Society.*

It is a great thing for members of the United Reformed Church to belong to a Church which has through its missions done so much to make the World Church a reality. It may still be a small Church, but it has helped to bring a very great family into being.

ECUMENICAL WORK It is not only a Church with many missionary heroes in the past. It has had some great leaders in the great world-wide unity movement of this century – the ecumenical movement. One of the general secretaries of the World Council of Churches, when it was coming into being (and one of the greatest of missionary statesmen) was an English Presbyterian, William Paton (1886–1943). Brought up in the same Church was Lesslie Newbigin (b. 1909), one of the first bishops of the united Church of South India, and one of the greatest missionary leaders in this generation.

The Congregational side of the inheritance produced Leslie Cooke (1908–67), a superbly inspiring preacher. As a young man he preached the hope of the gospel as bombs destroyed the centre of Coventry where he worked, and he later led the whole work of the World Council of Churches in helping the refugees and victims of disaster the world over. It was a Congregational minister, too, who lived long enough to become a minister of the United Reformed Church, who led one of the greatest common enterprises of the Churches in our day – the production of the New English Bible. Dr C. H. Dodd (1884–1974) was one of the most famous New Testament scholars of the world. He was the first Free churchman to be a divinity professor at Cambridge since Oliver Cromwell's day. It was only after he retired from being a professor that he took on the task of directing the production of this work: the first new translation of the Bible to be made officially by the Churches together since the reign of James I. Despite this late start in his life he lived long enough to see it finished, and his slight, ramrod-like figure marched up the aisle of Westminster Abbey to give the first copy to the Archbishop of Canterbury. He was then 88.

WORSHIP   It can be seen, then, that those who came into the United Reformed Church entered into a wonderful inheritance. This was not only true in the realms of missionary and ecumenical work and scholarship. It was true in one supreme instance in the realm of worship. Arguments will go on for ever among hymn lovers, about whether Isaac Watts or Charles Wesley was the greatest of English hymn writers. Perhaps we may say that they breast the tape together! Isaac Watts (1674–1748) was a Congregationalist, and he was really the pioneer of the English hymn. Until then the psalms alone were sung in most services. Watts set out to 'Christianise' the psalms. 'O God our help in ages past' sung on every Remembrance Day, is one result. (Watts based it on Psalm 90: he wrote '*Our* God', by the way.) One of the wonderful things about his great hymns is the way in which he constantly looks out to the large world of space and time. It makes his hymns fit our space-age times very well. Some of his words have enriched the English tongue wherever it is spoken. Think of 'When I survey the wondrous cross', 'There is a land of pure delight', and 'Jesus shall reign where'er the sun'.

The gift of hymn writing has certainly not died out. Perhaps the best known of all present-day hymn writers is Fred Kaan (b. 1929), a Dutchman who became an English Congregational minister. His hymns, very much in the language and idiom of today, are sung in many English-speaking lands. In the new hymn book of the two largest Protestant churches in Canada there are more of his hymns than of any other living writer.

One of the first things that the new Church did was to produce a small hymn book of its own, *New Church Praise*, not to replace the hymn books now in use, but to supplement them with hymns about the needs of today, written chiefly by writers of today. Many are by members

Revd Isaac Watts D.D.

Engraved by S. Freeman

of the United Reformed Church. One of the finest of our hymn writers is Brian Wren (b. 1936) whose hymns, again, will be found in many new collections.

So this chapter shows that as well as receiving a very good inheritance from the two Churches that united, the new Church has gone on to try to build on it. Its hope is that it will be building up an even better inheritance to bring to any larger union which may come about. The greatest day in the life of the United Reformed Church will be when it exists no longer, but when its life will flow into that of a much larger Church.

Think about . . .

Try to find out about the missionaries mentioned in this chapter, and other modern missionary work. Is there a place in the modern world for mission?

Look up in a hymn book some of Watts's hymns. Do you feel that his words, written in the eighteenth century, still have meaning for Christians today?

What kind of things do you think the modern Church wants to sing and praise God about? Are they different from the subjects in older hymns? Try to borrow a copy of *New Church Praise* and look at the new hymns.

Important Dates

1536   John Calvin begins his work in Geneva from which his side of the Reformation, and Presbyterianism are to spring.

1582   Robert Browne publishes books which set out Congregational principles.

1646   The Westminster Confession of Faith completed. The work of divines meeting in Westminster Abbey, this is the great statement of Presbyterian belief.

1658   The Savoy Declaration, a great statement of Congregational principles, is drawn up by representatives of 120 churches meeting in the chapel of the old Savoy Palace.

1662   The Act of Uniformity makes it illegal for Congregational, Baptist and Presbyterian ministers to stay in the Church of England.

1689   The Toleration Act gives Nonconformists some legal rights.

1795   The London Missionary Society is founded.

1832	The Congregational Union of England and Wales is formed.
1844	Some Presbyterian churches form the Presbyterian Church in England, and a foreign mission is founded.
1876	A wider union of Presbyterian churches forms the Presbyterian Church of England.
1951	An attempt at union between the Congregational Union of England and Wales and the Presbyterian Church of England fails, but a covenant is made between the two assemblies that the two Churches will work together.
1966	The Congregational Church in England and Wales is formed.
1966	The London Missionary Society becomes the Congregational Council for World Mission.
1972	The United Reformed Church comes into being by the union of the Congregational Church in England and Wales and the Presbyterian Church of England.

Further Reading

Because the United Reformed Church is so recently formed it has not yet had books written about it. *The United Reformed Church: A Historical Introduction* (25p) and *A Book of Order for Worship* (25p) are available from the Tavistock Bookroom, 86 Tavistock Place, London WC1H 9RT. From the same address copies can still be obtained of *The Scheme of Union* (20p), which brought the new church into being.

The English Free Churches by HORTON DAVIES (Home University Library: Oxford University Press) and *The Free Church Tradition in the Life of England* by E. A. PAYNE (S.C.M. Press) are excellent on the wider historical background.

Useful Addresses

The offices of the United Reformed Church are at United Reformed Church House, 86 Tavistock Place, London WC1H 9RT.

At the same address is the Tavistock Bookroom, which sells books and booklets about the work of the Church and the monthly magazine *Reform*.

Also there are the library and museum of the United Reformed Church Historical Society.

The Council for World Mission (Congregational and Reformed) has its headquarters at Livingstone House, 11 Carteret Street, London SW1H 9DL.